Original title:
The Starry Path to Sleep

Copyright © 2024 Creative Arts Management OÜ
All rights reserved.

Author: Ethan Prescott
ISBN HARDBACK: 978-9916-90-814-3
ISBN PAPERBACK: 978-9916-90-815-0

Whispers of the Midnight Skies

In the hush of night, secrets weave,
Stars murmur softly, never to leave.
The moon casts shadows, cool and bright,
As dreams take flight in silver light.

Breeze carries tales from the past,
Of whispered wishes, spells that last.
The cosmos dances, a gentle sway,
Guiding lost hearts on their way.

A Journey Through Celestial Dreams

On stardust trails, we wander far,
Each twinkling light, a guiding star.
Through cosmic realms, we drift and glide,
In the embrace of the night, we bide.

Nebulas bloom in colors bright,
Painting the canvas of the night.
With each breath, we capture time,
In dreams dipped in celestial rhyme.

Dreams Dipped in Starlight

In the quiet glow of midnight's kiss,
Dreams shimmer softly, a fleeting bliss.
Wrapped in a lullaby, we close our eyes,
Chasing wonders beneath starlit skies.

Each twinkle a story, a wish we send,
To the vast universe, our hopes transcend.
As galaxies spin, we lose our fears,
Finding our solace through whispered years.

A Journey Through Celestial Dreams

On stardust trails, we wander far,
Each twinkling light, a guiding star.
Through cosmic realms, we drift and glide,
In the embrace of the night, we bide.

Nebulas bloom in colors bright,
Painting the canvas of the night.
WIth each breath, we capture time,
In dreams dipped in celestial rhyme.

Dreams Dipped in Starlight

In the quiet glow of midnight's kiss,
Dreams shimmer softly, a fleeting bliss.
Wrapped in a lullaby, we close our eyes,
Chasing wonders beneath starlit skies.

Each twinkle a story, a wish we send,
To the vast universe, our hopes transcend.
As galaxies spin, we lose our fears,
Finding our solace through whispered years.

Moonlit Meanderings

Beneath the moon, the world transforms,
Peace envelops, and calmness warms.
With every step on the dew-kissed ground,
Nature's symphony becomes profound.

Echoes of night sing sweet refrains,
Where tranquility in darkness reigns.
Through winding paths and silver beams,
We traverse the landscape of our dreams.

A Lull in the Cosmic Dance

Stars whisper softly, a gentle breeze,
The moon hangs low, draped in peace.
Galaxies pause, in a hushed embrace,
Time stands still in this sacred space.

In the silence, planets align,
Waves of serenity, a heart's design.
Comets drift, tracing arcs of light,
In this stillness, we're wrapped so tight.

Nebulae sigh in colors so bright,
Embracing the calm of a starry night.
The universe breathes, a rhythmic chant,
A lull in the cosmic dance, we grant.

Moments linger in the stellar flow,
Each heartbeat synchronized with the glow.
In unity, we find our place,
A tranquil journey through endless space.

Comfort Found in the Night's Glow

Beneath the stars, a soft light spills,
Filling the dark with serene thrills.
Whispers of dreams on the cool night air,
Finding solace in moments rare.

The glow of the moon, a tender guide,
Cradling hearts where secrets hide.
Gentle shadows dance on the ground,
In the night's embrace, love is found.

Crickets serenade a soothing song,
Echoing truths where we belong.
Wrapped in comfort, the world fades away,
In the night's glow, we choose to stay.

Each breath a promise, each sigh a prayer,
In this quiet space, we lay bare.
Finding warmth in the starlit embrace,
Comfort lives here, in this sacred place.

Embrace of the Cosmos

In swirling depths of night, they shine,
Stars whisper secrets, divine.
Galaxies dance in cosmic grace,
An endless void, a timeless space.

Drifting through time, the starlight glows,
Illuminating paths that nobody knows.
Infinite wonders, vast and wide,
In the universe's arms, we abide.

Slumber's Guiding Light

When darkness drapes the world in peace,
A gentle glow helps worries cease.
Dreams take flight on silver beams,
In the realm where nothing seems.

Softly cradled in arms of night,
Whispers guide us toward the light.
In every shadow, hope is found,
As starry visions swirl around.

Twinkling Twilight Dreams

As day bids night a soft goodbye,
Twilight's canvas paints the sky.
With every hue, our spirits soar,
In dreams that whisper evermore.

Gentle breezes hum a tune,
Underneath the watchful moon.
In this embrace of fading light,
Our hearts take flight into the night.

Slumber's Guiding Light

When darkness drapes the world in peace,
A gentle glow helps worries cease.
Dreams take flight on silver beams,
In the realm where nothing seems.

Softly cradled in arms of night,
Whispers guide us toward the light.
In every shadow, hope is found,
As starry visions swirl around.

Twinkling Twilight Dreams

As day bids night a soft goodbye,
Twilight's canvas paints the sky.
With every hue, our spirits soar,
In dreams that whisper evermore.

Gentle breezes hum a tune,
Underneath the watchful moon.
In this embrace of fading light,
Our hearts take flight into the night.

Navigating the Nebula

Through nebulae, our ship will glide,
In colors rich, where wonders hide.
Cosmic currents pull us near,
As mysteries unfold, there's nothing to fear.

Stars like lanterns dot the way,
Guiding us until the break of day.
In the vastness, we discover grace,
Lost in the beauty of space's embrace.

Constellation Carriers

Beneath the vast, embracing sky,
We dance with lights that never die.
Stars like jewels in endless flight,
Carriers of our dreams at night.

With every flicker, tales they weave,
Of distant worlds, we dare believe.
Guiding hearts through cosmic streams,
Constellations cradle whispered dreams.

Infinite Nightfall

In the hush of twilight's sigh,
The universe begins to cry.
Shadows stretch across the ground,
Infinite nightfall, softly found.

Whispers of stars in silence seep,
Guard the secrets of those who sleep.
Wrapped in dark, we find our peace,
In this realm where worries cease.

Whispering Dreams of the Cosmos

Through velvet skies where comets race,
Whispers of dreams in boundless space.
Galaxies spin in graceful arcs,
Each twinkling light a fleeting spark.

Voices carried on solar winds,
Echo the tales of ancient sins.
In quiet moments, stars will share,
The mysteries found in cosmic air.

Lost Among the Stars

In the silence where shadows dwell,
I roam the night's enchanting spell.
Dreams drift softly, like dust in air,
Lost among the stars, I wander there.

Each shimmer holds a forgotten tale,
Guiding me through the cosmic veil.
Though I search for a way back home,
In this vastness, my heart will roam.

Starry Echoes

Whispers of the skies, so bright,
Echoing dreams through the night.
Stars collide in a cosmic dance,
Drawing hearts in a glance.

Galaxies twirl, they intertwine,
In the quiet, the stars align.
Silent stories in twinkling light,
Guiding travelers, lost in flight.

Each flicker holds a timeless tale,
A spark of hope in the vast veil.
Constellations draw maps on high,
Leading souls where wonders lie.

In the hush of night, we find,
Echoes resonate, intertwined.
With every star, a wish is cast,
In the sky, the dreams are vast.

Luminary Lullaby

Gentle glows in twilight's grip,
Moonbeams sing on the water's slip.
Shadows dance beneath the trees,
Nature hums with a tranquil ease.

Crickets chirp in harmony,
A symphony of night, so free.
Stars begin their soft parade,
While sleepy eyes in dreams are laid.

Breezes carry the sweet refrain,
Lullabies whispered in the rain.
Waves lap softly at the shore,
As night unfolds to the quiet core.

Rest now, dear heart, the night is still,
The world sleeps on, as dreams fulfill.
In this peace, let worries fly,
Beneath the watchful, velvet sky.

Cosmic Reflections

Mirrors in the sky reflect,
Secrets of the stars collect.
Infinite realms in their glow,
Mapping paths we long to know.

Planets spin with graceful might,
Dancing shadows, stealing light.
Nebulas bloom in vibrant hue,
Over cosmic seas, vast and blue.

Time flows differently up there,
Moments caught in starry snare.
We ponder life from our small earth,
In each spark, we trace our worth.

Cosmic dust, the birth of dreams,
Boundless wonders, endless themes.
In stillness, we dare to gaze,
Finding truth in the starlit maze.

Ethereal Night Odyssey

On a path of twilight hues,
Wanderers chase the evening blues.
Stars above, a guide of fire,
We follow dreams, hearts full of desire.

Through the wisps of misty air,
The universe calls, tender and rare.
Voices echo in the wide expanse,
In timeless rhythm, we sway and dance.

Galaxies twinkle, ancient and wise,
Telling tales that never die.
Every journey finds its way,
In the dance of night, come what may.

Ethereal realms of night ignite,
Illuminating the paths of light.
Together we roam, hand in hand,
On this cosmic, enchanted land.

Dreamlit Trails

In twilight's glow, the shadows dance,
Softly weaving dreams in trance.
A whispering breeze through rustling leaves,
Guides the heart where wonder weaves.

Each step upon the velvet ground,
Echoes tales of the lost and found.
Moonlit paths where secrets dwell,
In the heart where stories tell.

The stars above begin to shine,
Illuminating thoughts divine.
Chasing echoes of the night,
In a world of soft, silver light.

Through dreamlit trails, we wander free,
Unfolding magic, you and me.
A journey painted in hues of gold,
Where every step ignites the bold.

Celestial Whispers

Between the stars, where silence breathes,
Celestial whispers float like leaves.
Softly they call, like distant chimes,
Guiding hearts through the threads of time.

In twilight's hold, the cosmos sings,
Of ancient tales and forgotten things.
Beneath the moon's enchanting gaze,
We dance in dreams, lost in a haze.

Every twinkle, a story spun,
Of lovers, battles, lost and won.
In the stillness, secrets flow,
As stardust dances, soft and slow.

Through cosmic seas, our spirits soar,
In whispers of light, we seek to explore.
The universe cradles hopes and fears,
In the silent language of endless years.

Nocturnal Sojourn

In shadows deep, where silence lies,
The night unfolds beneath dark skies.
With every step, the world feels near,
In the quiet, all becomes clear.

Moonbeams weave through branches tall,
Casting silver spells over all.
A nocturnal sojourn, hearts aligned,
Through whispered secrets, souls entwined.

The rustle of leaves, a ghostly breath,
In nature's arms, we find our depth.
Starlit paths guide our way,
As dreams and shadows softly play.

Each moment holds a timeless grace,
In every corner, an embrace.
With dawn's approach, we linger still,
In this sojourn, our hearts shall fill.

Stardust Dreams

In a canvas of night where wishes gleam,
We chase the magic of stardust dreams.
With every heartbeat, a galaxy spins,
In vibrant hues, where adventure begins.

Whispers of hope in the cosmic flow,
Guiding our paths as we ebb and glow.
Through realms unknown, our spirits rise,
Dancing beneath the vast, open skies.

Together we twirl in the endless space,
Each moment we're lost in this sacred place.
With laughter and light, we paint the night,
In shimmering echoes of pure delight.

Stardust dreams, forever bright,
In the heart's embrace, we find our light.
A journey of wonder, hand in hand,
In the tapestry of dreams, we stand.

Celestial Comfort

In twilight's hush, the stars ignite,
Whispers of night, a soft delight.
Moonbeams dance on tranquil seas,
A cradle formed of cosmic ease.

Serenades of silence sway,
Guiding dreams that drift away.
Gentle winds tell tales of old,
In starlit hearts, the night unfolds.

Galaxies weave a soothing song,
In their embrace, we all belong.
Mysteries wrapped in velvet skies,
Comfort found where starlight lies.

With every breath, the universe sighs,
A symphony where our spirit flies.
Celestial peace, quietly we seek,
In the night's arms, our souls speak.

Starlit Reveries

Beneath the vast, eternal dome,
Stars ignite, a celestial home.
Each twinkle holds a whispered dream,
In the night, where hopes redeem.

Drifting thoughts like clouds above,
Caught in the light, the warmth of love.
Moonlit paths where wishes roam,
In starlit reveries, we find our own.

Timeless echoes of ancient lore,
Guide our hearts to distant shores.
Dreams take flight on comet's tail,
In space's arms, we shall not fail.

Amidst the velvet deep we dive,
In the glow of night, we feel alive.
Every star a flicker of grace,
In starlit spaces, we find our place.

Cosmic Serenity

In the hush of the galactic sea,
Cosmic whispers flow gently free.
Stars embrace the velvet night,
Guiding souls with their soft light.

Echoing through the silence vast,
Moments captured, shadows cast.
Contain the beauty, the peace we find,
In cosmic serenity, hearts unwind.

Nebulas swirl in colors bright,
Painting dreams in shades of light.
Floating softly on stardust streams,
Awash with hope, we weave our dreams.

Every twinkle a tale of old,
Stories of warmth yet to be told.
In the cosmos, our spirits soar,
Finding solace forevermore.

Napping in the Nebula

Drifting softly in twilight's embrace,
Napping gently in a starry place.
Colors blend in a cosmic fold,
A tapestry of dreams unfolds.

Nebulae whisper secrets sweet,
Cradled in stardust, we find our seat.
Every breath a lullaby's sound,
In the universe, peace is found.

Floating through realms of endless night,
We savor the magic, pure delight.
As constellations twinkle near,
In the cosmos, there's nothing to fear.

Dreamers drift on a cosmic ride,
In the nebula, hearts open wide.
With every heartbeat, freedom's song,
In the galaxy's arms, we belong.

Celestial Constellations

In the dark expanse, they gleam,
Whispers of stories, a timeless theme.
Connecting the dots, a cosmic thread,
Guiding the lost, where dreams are fed.

Stars like gems, so bright and rare,
Sketching our fate in the night air.
Each twinkle a promise, a fate entwined,
In the vastness where wonders bind.

Galaxies spin in a graceful dance,
Drawing our hearts in a knowing glance.
The universe sings in radiant hues,
In the heart of night, inspiration brews.

Lost in the gaze of their ancient light,
We find our stories, we take flight.
Celestial wonders, forever they stay,
In the ever-revolving night display.

Softer Than Starlight

Whispers of dusk in twilight's embrace,
Ethereal touch, a gentle trace.
Softer than starlight, dreams take wing,
Echoes of love that the night does bring.

Veils of silence drape the night,
In shadows, your spirit feels so light.
Every heartbeat, a soothing rhyme,
As we dance through the fabric of time.

Gentle breezes carry sweet sighs,
As moonbeams shimmer in your eyes.
Secrets rustle in the cool night air,
Reminders that magic is always there.

In the realm where dreams reside,
We find solace, hearts open wide.
Softer than starlight, love's sighs unfold,
Tales of a journey, in whispers told.

Elysian Dreams

In gardens of hope, where wishes bloom,
Elysian dreams dispel all gloom.
Harmony flows like a gentle stream,
In the embrace of a perfect dream.

Fragrant blossoms in the morning glow,
Stories of sunshine in every throw.
Butterflies dance, so light and free,
Whispering secrets between you and me.

Clouds of silk, where the stars align,
Each moment a treasure, purely divine.
We walk hand in hand, with hearts aglow,
In the realm of dreams, where love can grow.

Together we weave a tapestry bright,
Crafting our world in the tender night.
Elysian dreams, a sweet serenade,
In every heartbeat, our love displayed.

Cosmic Choreography

In the cosmic ballet, the stars collide,
A timeless dance, where dreams abide.
Galaxies spiral, galaxies swirl,
In the vastness, mysteries unfurl.

Planets align in a graceful arc,
Igniting the darkness, igniting the sparks.
Every motion a script, a celestial play,
Where stardust whispers and comets sway.

Dancers of light, in beautiful flight,
Painting the canvas of infinite night.
Each step a story, each turn a song,
In cosmic choreography, where we belong.

With every heartbeat, the universe hums,
Echoes of love as the cosmos drums.
In this grand design, we find our place,
In the dance of the stars, we share our grace.

The Slumber of Astral Waves

In the cradle of stars, so softly they sway,
Whispers of dusk weave a tapestry gray.
Lulled by the tide of the cosmic night's call,
Hearts drift in silence, as shadows enthrall.

Gentle are breezes that kiss the dark air,
Melodies murmur, a tranquil affair.
Galaxies twinkle, winking with grace,
In dreams we wander, lost in this space.

Moonbeams are lullabies, wrapped in their glow,
Guiding the wanderers where star rivers flow.
The slumber of night, a celestial song,
We cradle the stillness where spirits belong.

Dreams Swaddled in Twilight's Embrace

Veils of soft twilight, drape over the sea,
Whispers of dreams float on winds, wild and free.
Cradled in shadows, the world lays forlorn,
In twilight's embrace, the new day is born.

Stars flicker gently, like fireflies at play,
Chasing the echoes of night into day.
In moments of silence, the heart learns to soar,
Finding the magic on the twilight's shore.

Resting in stillness, we savor the hour,
The hush that envelops, a magical power.
In dreams swaddled softly, we find our own song,
In twilight's embrace, we finally belong.

Celestial Gardens of Rest

In gardens of starlight, where shadows bloom,
Flowers of stardust dispel all the gloom.
Petals of moonlight dance soft on the breeze,
Whispers of dreams lull the soul with such ease.

Crickets are choristers, singing at night,
Guiding our thoughts to the world of pure light.
In the calm of the heavens, our spirits take flight,
Through celestial gardens, we wander till bright.

Nestled in colors, where time drifts away,
In the hush of the night, our worries decay.
With each breath we take, we awaken our rest,
In celestial gardens, the heart feels blessed.

Nightfall's Embrace of Light

As day turns to night, a soft cloak descends,
The sun bids farewell, as twilight transcends.
Stars bloom above, like flowers aglow,
In nightfall's embrace, the world moves slow.

Deep shadows entwine with a glimmer of gold,
Stories unfold as the cosmos grows bold.
In whispers of night, where dreams intertwine,
We dance with the galaxies, partner divine.

Awash in the beauty of soft silver beams,
We gather the fragments of luminous dreams.
In the still of the night, with hearts full of light,
We sway with the stardust, our spirits take flight.

Moonbeam Lullabies

In the quiet night, stars gleam bright,
Whispers of dreams take gentle flight.
Moonbeams dance on silver streams,
Cradling the world in soft moonbeams.

Lullabies sung to the sleepy trees,
Carried aloft on a tender breeze.
Dreamers drift on clouds of white,
Wrapped in the magic of the night.

Cosmic Comforts

Across the sky, where stardust flows,
Galaxies twinkle, a soft repose.
Nebulas bloom in colors bold,
Embracing wanderers, tales retold.

In the vastness, hearts find calm,
Wrapped in the universe's balm.
Silent echoes of love's refrain,
Bringing solace through the cosmic plane.

Velvet Skies

Velvet skies blanket the world below,
Whispers of night in a gentle glow.
Stars like diamonds, a treasure trove,
Inviting hearts to dream and rove.

The moon hangs low, a watchful eye,
Guiding the dreams that wander by.
Cradled in night's tender embrace,
Time slows down in this sacred space.

Silent Nights

In the silence, secrets unfold,
Stories of ages quietly told.
Time stands still as shadows dance,
Lost in the night's enchanting trance.

The world asleep, yet hearts awake,
In every breath, a new chance to take.
Silence sings a soothing tune,
Cradled beneath the watching moon.

Wanderlust in the Milky Way

Under the stars, dreams take flight,
Painting the canvas of the night.
With every step, a journey new,
The Milky Way calls, inviting you.

Clouds of wonder, spices of time,
Echoes of laughter, a soft chime.
Wanderlust beckons, a siren's song,
Together we'll roam where we belong.

Silent Nights

In the silence, secrets unfold,
Stories of ages quietly told.
Time stands still as shadows dance,
Lost in the night's enchanting trance.

The world asleep, yet hearts awake,
In every breath, a new chance to take.
Silence sings a soothing tune,
Cradled beneath the watching moon.

Wanderlust in the Milky Way

Under the stars, dreams take flight,
Painting the canvas of the night.
With every step, a journey new,
The Milky Way calls, inviting you.

Clouds of wonder, spices of time,
Echoes of laughter, a soft chime.
Wanderlust beckons, a siren's song,
Together we'll roam where we belong.

Nocturnal Embrace

In shadows deep, the night does sigh,
Stars twinkle softly in the sky.
A gentle breeze whispers your name,
In this dark world, we are the same.

Clad in dreams, we drift like smoke,
Under the hush, our hearts bespoke.
The moon casts light on paths unknown,
In silence shared, we are not alone.

A dance of flickers, the fireflies glow,
Time suspends, in love's gentle flow.
Wrapped in warmth, we close our eyes,
As magic weaves through starry ties.

Through every murmur, nightbirds call,
In nocturnal embrace, we fall.
With every heartbeat soft and clear,
In dreams entwined, forever near.

Restful Whispers of the Night

Beneath the stars, a hush prevails,
The moonlight dances, softly trails.
In velvet night, the world unwinds,
Restful whispers drift through minds.

Crickets serenade the gentle breeze,
Rustling leaves sing through the trees.
A tender peace embraces all,
In restful whispers, we heed the call.

Dreams take flight on wings of calm,
Wrapped in scents of night's perfume balm.
Each breath a lullaby, sweet and light,
Guiding souls through the tranquil night.

In silver shadows, we find our way,
Through twilight's veil, into the gray.
Let worries fade, just hold me tight,
In the soft arms of the night.

Moonlit Musings

Under the spell of the silvery moon,
Thoughts cascade like petals in June.
Each glow a story waiting to be told,
In the night's embrace, we break the mold.

Reflections dance on rivers wide,
In moonlit musings, dreams abide.
The world a canvas of shadows and light,
Painting our souls with a touch so bright.

Wander through echoes of time and space,
In the serene glow, we find our place.
Every moment a treasure, a silent delight,
Under the watch of stars, this beautiful night.

Let whispers of wisdom guide us near,
In the heart of the night, there's nothing to fear.
With every twinkle, a thought takes flight,
In the chamber of dreams, we revel in light.

Dreams Adrift in Space

Floating softly in the cosmic sea,
Where stardust mingles, wild and free.
Dreams adrift on celestial streams,
In the vast expanse, we weave our dreams.

Galaxies shimmer, a magical show,
Whispers of worlds we long to know.
With every heartbeat, we chase the stars,
In the embrace of night, we forget our scars.

Time unravels, a silver thread,
In dreams' embrace, we are widely spread.
Together we wander, lost yet found,
In the vastness of night, where love knows no bound.

As nebulas glow in a silent dance,
Every heartbeat, a cosmic chance.
In dreams adrift, we touch the sky,
In the dream of the night, we learn to fly.

Tranquil Moments Beneath the Sky

In the hush of twilight's glow,
Whispers of nature softly flow.
Stars begin to blink and gleam,
As night unfolds a serene dream.

Gentle breezes weave through trees,
Carrying scents of sweet release.
Moonlight spills on silent ground,
A soothing presence all around.

Crickets sing their lullabies,
While shadows dance in soft replies.
Each heartbeat slows, a peaceful sigh,
In tranquil moments 'neath the sky.

With every glance at starlit skies,
Wonder ignites, and spirit flies.
In these still moments, I find peace,
Nature's magic, a sweet release.

Celestial Conclusions

Stars align with whispered grace,
In the night's embrace, we trace.
A tapestry of dreams unfurled,
In celestial dance, we're twirled.

Planets wander, paths entwine,
Stories written in the divine.
As comets blaze across the dark,
Hope ignites a brilliant spark.

Through cosmic realms, we drift and soar,
Seeking truths that lie in lore.
Each glance up holds a fleeting chance,
In the universe, we find our dance.

Galaxies whisper tales untold,
Of love and loss, of brave and bold.
In every twinkle, secrets live,
Celestial conclusions, the night can give.

A Journey Through the Night

Beneath the moon's soft silver light,
We venture forth into the night.
Footfalls quiet on the ground,
A melody of peace is found.

Stars above like scattered dreams,
Guiding us with gentle beams.
Each shadow tells a tale anew,
As we wander, just me and you.

The air is thick with mystery,
A canvas rich with history.
In this journey, hearts unite,
As we weave through paths of twilight.

With every step, our worries fade,
In the night's embrace, we wade.
Together, hand in hand, we trust,
On this journey of love, we must.

Underneath the Milky Canopy

Beneath the vast and milky sheen,
We lie and gaze at worlds unseen.
Galaxies swirl in silent flight,
As dreams unfold in cosmic night.

The universe wraps us in its arms,
A tapestry of hidden charms.
Each star a wish, a hope, a plea,
In this celestial symphony.

Crickets serenade the evening air,
While fireflies weave a dance so rare.
Underneath this radiant dome,
We find in darkness, our true home.

With whispered thoughts that drift like smoke,
In this moment, words evoke,
The beauty found in silence deep,
Underneath the Milky canopy.

Sleep's Journey Through the Ether

In shadows deep, where silence creeps,
The weary head will slowly bow.
A velvet night, the promise keeps,
Embracing dreams, the heart allows.

With every breath, the world does fade,
In softest wisps, the spirit flies.
To distant lands of light and shade,
Where whispers float and laughter sighs.

Through cosmic paths, the visions soar,
On starlit wings, our thoughts take flight.
Unraveled fears, we meet once more,
In realms unseen, beyond the night.

The ether's grasp, a warm caress,
With every pulse, the heartbeats hum.
In slumber's hold, we find our rest,
As dreams unfold, a world become.

Celestial Reveries and Stardust Sighs

A canvas painted, skies so wide,
With echoes of a lullaby.
In twilight's glow, the stars abide,
Their glimmer calling, "Come, comply."

Beneath the moon's soft, silver sheen,
The secrets of the night take form.
With whispers sweet, in shadows keen,
We dance among the starlit swarm.

Each twinkle weaves a tale untold,
Of lost desires and dreams reborn.
In every glance, new sparks unfold,
As stardust trails the paths we mourn.

With every sigh, the night retrieves,
The hopeful hearts that dare to glow.
In celestial realms, our spirit weaves,
A tapestry of love bestowed.

Constellation Comforts and Kindred Dreams

Among the night, where shadows weave,
The constellations whisper low.
In twilight's hush, we learn to believe,
That dreams can flourish, softly grow.

The bear, the hunter, stories told,
In cosmic depths, we lose our fear.
Each star a friend, with light of gold,
Their presence draws our souls so near.

In gatherings of kindred hearts,
The galaxy becomes our guide.
With every gaze, a bond imparts,
Connecting worlds where love won't hide.

To navigate the night's embrace,
With constellations, hand in hand.
In dreams transformed, we find our place,
Together in this timeless land.

Wandering Through the Midnight Glow

In midnight's glow, our spirits roam,
Through valleys deep and hills so high.
The echoing whispers lead us home,
To lands where dreams and starlight lie.

Among the trees, the shadows play,
With glimmers twinkling in the air.
We follow paths where nightbirds sway,
With gentle hearts, we weave our prayer.

As constellations light the sky,
The mysteries of the dark unfold.
In every breath, a spark to fly,
To find the stories yet untold.

So wander forth, through midnight's grace,
Embrace the glow that softly calls.
For in this dance, we find our place,
Where every heartbeat softly falls.

The Horizon of Sleepy Stars

In the night, the stars gleam bright,
Whispers of dreams take their flight.
Soft shadows dance on the ground,
In this calm, peace is found.

The moon bathes the world in silver,
While gentle winds begin to sliver.
Each twinkle sings a lullaby,
As we gaze at the endless sky.

Fading echoes of the day,
Guide us gently on our way.
With eyes closed, we start to drift,
As the universe begins to lift.

In the horizon, slumber stays,
Enfolding us in twilight's haze.
With sleepy stars our hearts align,
In the embrace of night divine.

Softly Woven in Twilight's Veil

Veils of dusk softly descend,
As day and night begin to blend.
In the hush, colors fade away,
Wrapping dreams in shades of gray.

Stars awaken, one by one,
Painting heavens, dusk begun.
A tapestry of light unfolds,
Cradling secrets that night holds.

Gentle breezes, whispers low,
Carry tales of dreams that flow.
In twilight's touch, hearts can mend,
Hope is woven, never ends.

Drifting softly, let us roam,
In this twilight, we find home.
With every breath, we start anew,
In the magic of the blue.

Echoes of Stars in Quietude

Stars cast their echoes in the night,
In the stillness, a serene sight.
With every flicker, a story shared,
In the void, we feel prepared.

Silence falls like a gentle sigh,
As constellations softly lie.
In the vastness, dreams ignite,
Guiding us through endless light.

Each heartbeat joins the cosmic tune,
Under the watchful gaze of the moon.
As shadows blend and worlds unite,
We find our place in the starlit night.

With quietude, our souls take flight,
Echoing whispers of unspoken might.
In the embrace of the rhythm, we see,
The endless dance of what can be.

Tranquil Steps on Cosmic Sands

Footprints trace upon the sands,
In the stillness, time expands.
Endless cosmos stretches wide,
With each step, the stars abide.

Glistening grains catch the light,
A symphony of day and night.
Softly echoing the dreams we seek,
In the silence, the universe speaks.

As we wander, hearts aligned,
Cosmic wonders intertwined.
With tranquil steps, we roam afar,
Guided by the northern star.

In the vast, where dreams are planned,
We find magic in cosmic sand.
With every breath, we journey on,
In this boundless light, we belong.

Starman's Rest

In the quiet night sky, he dreams,
Whispers of cosmos in moonbeams.
Stars gather close, a soft embrace,
Each twinkle a promise, a glowing trace.

Rest now, brave soul, let worries cease,
In starlit slumber, find your peace.
Galaxies hum a lullaby sweet,
As celestial visions whisper and greet.

Eclipses and comets dance in flight,
Guiding lost travelers through the night.
With every breath, the heavens sigh,
For a starman, the universe is nigh.

So close your eyes to ride the gleam,
On wings of stardust, chase your dream.
Tomorrow brings wonders that some will see,
For in the cosmos, all can be free.

Prairie of Stars

Beneath the vast and endless dome,
A prairie of stars feels like home.
Whispers of winds in the midnight air,
Carrying stories of those who dare.

Each flicker a tale from times long past,
Shadows of dreams that will ever last.
Across the horizon, they silently gleam,
Lighting the path for each hopeful dream.

In the stillness of night, a canvas glows,
Fields of wishes where wild magic flows.
Feel the pulse of the earth, hold it tight,
The prairie of stars shines ever bright.

Dance with the fireflies, sway with the breeze,
Embrace the night, feel the gentle freeze.
In this meadow of light, we laugh and we cry,
For under the stars, our spirits can fly.

Dreaming the Universe

In the realm of night where shadows weave,
A tapestry bright, we dare to believe.
A dance of the stars in cosmic ballet,
Holding the secrets of night and day.

Floating on whispers of stellar streams,
We're drifting in circles, lost in our dreams.
Galaxies twirl, in a spiral spin,
With every heartbeat, the universe grins.

Time is a river, a flowing song,
Connecting the moments, where we belong.
With visions of wonder, we chase the light,
Dreaming the universe, taking flight.

So cast away doubts, embrace the unknown,
In the cosmic embrace, we are never alone.
For in dreaming the universe, we find our place,
A journey of stars, in infinite space.

Celestial Driftwood

Upon the shore of the endless sea,
Lies driftwood of starlight, wild and free.
Each piece a story, a whispering tale,
Carried by currents, in moonlight pale.

Waves of silver lap against the night,
Guiding the lost towards the light.
Celestial wonders, forever untold,
Each splinter of wood, a vision of gold.

Pulled by the tides of the cosmic swirl,
Hearts are awakened, dreams start to whirl.
With every splash, the universe calls,
As driftwood of starlight softly falls.

So gather your remnants, let them align,
In the dance of the cosmos, everything's fine.
For in the driftwood, we find our way,
A piece of the universe, come what may.

A Voyage to Dreamland

In the hush of night, we sail,
On feathered clouds, a gentle gale.
Whispers of dreams in the air,
Guiding us softly, without a care.

Stars above twinkle and gleam,
Leading us onward, lost in a dream.
With every breath, we drift anew,
To shores where the skies are painted blue.

The moonlight dances on calm seas,
Wrapped in the arms of a soft breeze.
Voices of childhood call us near,
In this land where nothing is unclear.

As dawn approaches, our journey ends,
Yet in our hearts, this magic blends.
Tomorrow awaits with tales to stream,
Another voyage, another dream.

Navigating Night's Canvas

Under a blanket of velvet night,
We sail through dreams, lost in delight.
Canvas of stars, twinkling bright,
Illuminating paths, guiding our flight.

Gentle waves murmur soft songs,
Whispers of wonder where we belong.
With each pull of the midnight tide,
Our hopes and dreams, in ripples, ride.

The moon paints silver on the ground,
In its glow, sweet mysteries abound.
Casting shadows, we dance and sway,
Lost in the night, come what may.

As horizons shift in the dark,
We find our way, igniting a spark.
With every stroke of night's embrace,
We navigate through time and space.

Starlight's Caress

In twilight's hush, the stars align,
With a soft touch, they intertwine.
Caressing dreams and whispered sighs,
Awakening worlds beneath dark skies.

Each flickering light, a story told,
Of love and loss, both brave and bold.
In their glimmer, we find our way,
Through veils of night, till break of day.

Gentle breezes carry our hopes,
On starlit paths, we learn to cope.
A guiding light in vast unknown,
Starlight's warmth feels like home.

As night lingers, we embrace the glow,
In starlight's caress, we freely flow.
With every heartbeat, dreams unfold,
In this cosmic dance, our spirits hold.

Shimmering Gateway to Dreams

Beyond the horizon, where the sun dips low,
Lies a shimmering path where the dreamers go.
With every step, the magic ignites,
Opening portals to endless nights.

Whispers of wonder paint skies in gold,
Stories of journeys yet to be told.
Each shimmering light, a promise to keep,
In the arms of the night, we drift deep.

The gateway beckons, a siren's call,
Enticing us gently, we're bound to fall.
Through gardens of slumber, we soar and glide,
In a world where the imagination can't hide.

As dawn approaches, the dreams may fade,
But memories linger, sweet serenade.
With hearts alight and souls aglow,
We cherish the magic in dreams we sow.

Starlit Silhouettes

In twilight's hush, silhouettes dance,
Whispers of dreams in a silent trance.
Beneath the stars, shadows take flight,
Embracing the magic of the night.

The moon drapes silver on every face,
Casting soft light in this hushed space.
With every twinkle, secrets unfold,
Of stories forgotten, and dreams retold.

A canvas vast, the night's embrace,
Each star a beacon, finding its place.
Drifting on wishes, hopes intertwine,
In starlit silhouettes, all feels divine.

As dawn approaches, a gentle sigh,
The night retreats, but does not die.
In morning's glow, memories soar,
Starlit silhouettes remain evermore.

Twilight's Gentle Touch

Twilight whispers, soft and low,
The world adorned in a warm glow.
Shadows stretch, the day bids farewell,
In twilight's grasp, all secrets dwell.

Colors blend in a painted sky,
As dreams awaken, and night draws nigh.
Each breath a melody, softly played,
In twilight's gentle touch, we wade.

Stars emerge, like diamonds bright,
Guiding lost souls through the night.
With every heartbeat, moments blend,
In twilight's embrace, time seems to bend.

As darkness falls, hearts feel free,
In the solace of night, we simply be.
Twilight's gentle touch, a fleeting glance,
A hush that invites us to take a chance.

Beyond the Horizon of Sleep

In dreams we wander, far and wide,
Beyond the horizon, where hopes reside.
Each slumbering thought a guiding star,
Leading us gently, no matter how far.

The night unfolds like pages turned,
In whispering shadows, our spirits yearned.
Time flows softly, like a gentle stream,
In the quiet of night, we dare to dream.

Through valleys of starlight, we drift away,
Where echoes of laughter and memories play.
Beyond the horizon, the heart takes flight,
Embraced by the magic that dances in night.

As dawn approaches, our dreams must yield,
Yet in our hearts, the night is sealed.
Beyond the horizon of sleep, we find,
A treasure of moments, forever entwined.

The Celestial Journey

Under the sky, vast and deep,
We embark on a journey, not for sleep.
Stars beckon brightly, a cosmic song,
Guiding our souls where we belong.

With every heartbeat, the universe sways,
In a dance of light through endless days.
Galaxies twirl in a timeless embrace,
The celestial journey, an endless chase.

Nebulas painted in colors so rare,
Whispering secrets in the cool air.
The vast unknown calls out to roam,
Across the cosmos, we find a home.

As we traverse through the starry sea,
The journey unfolds, wild and free.
In the heart of the night, we boldly fly,
The celestial journey, our spirits high.

Celestial Shadows and Silent Slumber

In velvet nights where shadows play,
The stars adorn the dark ballet.
Whispers of the cosmos call,
Inviting dreams to softly fall.

Beneath the moon's enchanting grace,
We find our peace, our sacred space.
Each sigh a lull, each breath a friend,
In silent slumber, time suspends.

The universe unfolds its lace,
As constellations weave their trace.
A gentle pull, the heart's retreat,
In dreams we roam, so complete.

As dawn approaches, shadows blend,
The night we loved must come to end.
Yet in our hearts, the echoes remain,
Of celestial dreams, our sweet refrain.

A Voyage Among the Glittering Abyss

Set sail upon the starlit sea,
Where galaxies whisper, wild and free.
In cosmic waves, our spirits soar,
Through glittering depths, forevermore.

Nebulae swirl in vibrant hues,
Secrets hidden in the cosmic blues.
Each spark a tale, a voyage grand,
Adventures waiting at our command.

Through blackened skies, we trace our flight,
Navigating realms of pure delight.
The abyss calls with its mystic song,
In this vast wonder, we belong.

Together drifting, hearts entwined,
In the universe, our souls aligned.
A dance of stars, a timeless bliss,
In the sparkling void, we find our kiss.

Nebulae Nurturing Night

Softly blooms the cosmic dawn,
As nebulae cradle worlds withdrawn.
In colors rich, they weave a tale,
Of whispered dreams in the night's veil.

Guardians of the starlit skies,
They hold our hopes, our gentle sighs.
Cradled in their vast embrace,
We find our thoughts in perfect space.

The midnight air, a lullaby,
As galaxies waltz in the velvet high.
Each twinkle tells of paths untrod,
In the cosmic dance, we find our nod.

Together we drift beneath their charms,
In nebulae's cradle, safe from harms.
The night nurtures, our spirits rise,
In this sanctuary, the soul replies.

Starlit Trails to Tranquility

Along the trails where silence sings,
The stars reveal their quiet wings.
Each glow a path, a guiding light,
Leading us gently through the night.

With every step on cosmic ground,
A melody of peace is found.
In tranquil hearts, the universe,
Whispers softly, a gentle verse.

Wrapped in shadows, dreams unfold,
As secrets of the night are told.
In starlit paths, our worries cease,
Finding refuge, a moment's peace.

As twilight fades, the dawn does call,
Yet in our hearts, the night stands tall.
The starlit trails, forever ours,
A dance beneath the cosmic stars.

Dreamscapes of the Night Sky

In velvet depths, the stars do play,
Whispers of dreams in shades of gray.
Nebulas swirl, a cosmic dance,
In night's embrace, we find our chance.

Winds of wonder gently blow,
Carrying secrets we yearn to know.
Floating on clouds of silver beams,
We sail within our deepest dreams.

Galaxies spin in silent grace,
In the vastness, we find our place.
Time stretches thin as shadows creep,
In the night sky, our hearts leap.

Each twinkling light, a distant song,
Guiding the way where souls belong.
Chasing the visions, bright and wide,
Through dreamscapes of the night sky, we ride.

Echoes of Light in Sleep

In the quiet hush of the night,
Echoes dance in beams of light.
Softly they call, like a gentle sigh,
Luring the weary to dream and fly.

Luminous trails of a twilight glow,
Whispers of stories we're yet to know.
They flutter and weave in slumber's hold,
In the canvas of night, their secrets unfold.

Reflections of hope in shadows deep,
Awaken the heart from restless sleep.
Each flickering beam, a tale to spin,
In echoes of light, new worlds begin.

Through the veil of dreams, we drift afar,
Guided by echoes, like a distant star.
In this realm where silence speaks,
We find the solace our spirit seeks.

Gentle Glimmers in the Dark

Amidst the depths where shadows lie,
Glimmers pulse like stars in the sky.
With every blink, a soft embrace,
Illuminating the hidden space.

Whispers of night with tender cheer,
Guide us with glimmers, oh so near.
They dance like fireflies, swift and free,
In the dark, they call to thee.

Each spark a story, a wish, a dream,
Shining brightly, a silver seam.
In the stillness, they weave their art,
Gentle glimmers, they warm the heart.

As darkness deepens, fears take flight,
With glimmers aglow, we find our light.
In the silent hours, let hope embark,
In the wonder of gentle glimmers dark.

Intergalactic Peace

In silence vast, the cosmos sighs,
Reflecting peace beyond the skies.
Stars, like candles, flicker bright,
In the tapestry of endless night.

Galactic whispers, soft and clear,
Promising calm that all can hear.
Uniting worlds with a tender beam,
Crafting peace in a timeless dream.

Nebulas cradle the weary heart,
Binding us close, though worlds apart.
Harmony flows through ether's space,
In intergalactic peace, we find grace.

Each shimmering path, a bridge we share,
In this journey, we show we care.
Together we soar, however far,
In the embrace of the universe's star.

Beneath a Canopy of Wishes

In twilight's glow, dreams take flight,
Whispers of hopes, soft as night.
Stars weave tales, both bright and bold,
Beneath the sky, hearts unfold.

Gentle breezes carry sighs,
Casting wishes to the skies.
Each flicker, a prayer sent,
Beneath the stars, our spirits lent.

Moonlight dances on silken streams,
Illuminating our quiet dreams.
With every twinkle, a chance to find,
A world where love and peace unwind.

As night enfolds, we hold our breath,
Beneath this sky, we feel no death.
Bound by the light of endless night,
In dreams, our wishes take their flight.

The Celestial Lullaby

Softly sings the twilight hour,
Stars awaken, shine, empower.
Moonbeams whisper a gentle tune,
Cradled by night, beneath the moon.

Clouds drift softly, cotton dreams,
Wrapped in silver, silent beams.
Each note a touch, both calm and sweet,
The celestial song, a lullaby treat.

As night stretches, shadows play,
Guiding souls along their way.
In the embrace of night so high,
We find our peace, we learn to fly.

Under the cosmos, hearts entwined,
In every star, our hopes aligned.
The universe hums a soft refrain,
In this lullaby, we remain.

Stardust Comforts the Soul

In the hush of night, stars descend,
Whispers of love, on which we depend.
Stardust glimmers in the cool air,
Reminding us that dreams still care.

With each spark, a memory glows,
Comforting hearts, where stillness flows.
Beneath the sky, we find our place,
In stardust trails, we leave our trace.

Gently wrapped in night's embrace,
The universe holds a warm space.
Drawing forth dreams from the deep,
In stardust's touch, we find our sleep.

So let the cosmos soothe your fears,
As stardust whispers through the years.
In every shimmer, a tale retold,
Comforts the soul with threads of gold.

Night's Tapestry of Radiance

In the fabric of night, colors weave,
Radiance glimmers, hopes believe.
Moonlight weaves through shadowed threads,
As dreams unfold, and courage spreads.

A tapestry rich with stories spun,
Of lost loves and victories won.
Each hue a smile, each shadow a tear,
In the night's embrace, we conquer fear.

Silhouettes dance in the soft moonbeam,
Painting our lives like a waking dream.
Through twilight whispers, we find our way,
In night's embrace, we choose to stay.

Stars twinkle bright in this woven night,
A canvas of dreams, a world of light.
With every heartbeat, we come alive,
In night's tapestry, our spirits thrive.

Resting Under a Canopy of Stars

Beneath the vast and twinkling night,
I find my peace, my heart takes flight.
The whispers of the breeze so low,
Guide my dreams where starlight flows.

The moon hangs bright, a silver sheen,
Illuminating all that's serene.
Each star a wish, a hope, a prayer,
In this embrace, I feel no care.

With every breath, the cosmos sighs,
As midnight paints the velvet skies.
In silence deep, my spirit's freed,
Together, lost in night's sweet creed.

Underneath this canvas grand,
I close my eyes, with dreams unplanned.
Held close by night, my heart will soar,
Resting here, forevermore.

Sleep's Infinite Journey

A journey starts when night descends,
Through whispered dreams and unseen bends.
With every sigh, the world fades slow,
Into the depths where shadows grow.

Time slips away in the starry trail,
Each moment woven in a silken veil.
I sail on clouds, through realms of night,
Chasing the dawn, the morning light.

In slumber deep, my spirit flies,
Past endless seas and distant skies.
Through echoes soft, I drift and sway,
In sleep's embrace, I lose my way.

Awake, I yearn for journeys vast,
To dive in dreams, holding them fast.
For in the night, my heart ignites,
On sleep's sweet journey, I find my rights.

Serenity in the Starlight

In quietude, the starlight glows,
Cradling secrets the night bestows.
Each flicker speaks of peace profound,
In the silence, beauty's found.

With gentle strokes, the moonlight paints,
A tranquil scene where nothing faints.
The world, it pauses, breathless, still,
Awash in calm, my soul to fill.

Wrapped in night's serene embrace,
I lose myself in this sacred space.
Whispers of the universe align,
In starlit peace, my heart is mine.

As dreams unfold like flowers rare,
I float on air, without a care.
In this moment, time stands by,
Serenity reigns beneath the sky.

Galaxies of Rest

In galaxies where night takes flight,
I wander through the depths of light.
Each star a beacon, bright and clear,
Guiding me to dreams held dear.

The Milky Way, a river wide,
Carries hopes where worlds abide.
In cosmic calm, my spirit glows,
Among the stars, my heart bestows.

With every breath, the cosmos breathes,
In restful arms, my soul receives.
Moments linger, soft and bright,
In galaxies of purest night.

So let me drift where starlight dances,
In boundless space, I find my chances.
For in these depths, forever blessed,
I find my peace, my heart at rest.

Pathway to the Celestial Garden

Beneath the blooms of starlit skies,
A winding path where dreamers rise.
With whispers soft, the night unfolds,
Each petal tells of tales untold.

In hues of gold and silver light,
The fragrance drifts through gentle night.
Where wishes dance upon the breeze,
And hearts embrace their memories.

The moonlight paints a tranquil glow,
As constellations tell us so.
A tranquil realm of peace and grace,
Here we find our sacred space.

In every step, a story grows,
Through garden paths, the spirit flows.
In harmony, we shall abide,
And walk this dream, our souls allied.

Embracing the Velvet Night

In shades of blue, the night reveals,
A cloak of quiet, soft as peels.
Stars twinkle like scattered dreams,
Lost in the hush of moonlit beams.

The gentle breeze, a lover's sigh,
As shadows dance beneath the sky.
We find our place, a secret nook,
Where time stands still, and hearts can look.

With velvet skies, we intertwine,
Our hopes alight, like fireflies shine.
In every glance, a universe,
A song etched deep, we shall converse.

Embracing night, we lose our fears,
In moments sweet, we shed our tears.
Together bound, our spirits soar,
In velvet night, we seek for more.

Sailing on a Sea of Stars

Upon the waves of twilight dreams,
We sail where starlight softly beams.
A journey vast, the cosmos calls,
With every wave, the mystery sprawls.

The constellations guide our way,
As time slips gently into play.
A vessel made from hopes and fears,
We navigate through time and years.

With each soft ripple, tales unfold,
Of journeys taken, stories bold.
A universe within our hearts,
As stardust weaves its ancient arts.

Across this sea, through night we glide,
With dreams and wishes as our guide.
In every moment's fleeting breath,
We find the warmth that conquers death.

The Cosmic Quilt

In fabric stitched from light and time,
Each patch a story, each seam a rhyme.
The universe in colors spun,
A tapestry where all are one.

With threads of fate, the stars align,
A cosmic quilt that feels divine.
Embracing all who wander near,
In patterns woven, bright and clear.

Galaxies twirl in playful dance,
Each stitch a moment, each line a chance.
Through shadows deep and radiant beams,
The quilt enfolds our deepest dreams.

As time unfolds, this quilt will grow,
In every heart, the love we sow.
Together stitched in harmony,
The cosmic quilt, our legacy.

Dreaming in the Milky Void

In the silence of the night,
Galaxies swirl in light.
Whispers dance on cosmic winds,
As my wandering soul transcends.

Floating through the endless dark,
Each star a brightened spark.
Nebulas cradle my weary mind,
In this realm, all dreams unwind.

Time drips slowly like the sky,
In this void, I learn to fly.
Cradled by the starlit stream,
I drift within a lucid dream.

Embracing all the mysteries,
With the universe, I find peace.
In the Milky Void's embrace,
I lose myself in endless space.

Guided by the Moon

Beneath a silver glow,
The night begins to flow.
With every shimmering beam,
I am lost within a dream.

Whispers of the night unfold,
Secrets waiting to be told.
The moon, a guardian bright,
Guides my heart through the night.

In shadows deep, I wander free,
With each step, more of me.
Underneath the celestial guide,
I embrace the cosmic tide.

A cosmic dance, a gentle sway,
With the moon, I find my way.
Her soft light a sweet embrace,
In her glow, I find my place.

Sleep's Interstellar Voyage

Drifting through the velvet sky,
Stars twinkle, a lullaby.
On this ship of dreams, I sail,
With the cosmos in my trail.

Galaxies spin, a wondrous sight,
A tapestry of the night.
Through the void, I softly glide,
In my heart, the stars abide.

The planets hum a soothing tune,
Cradled by the silver moon.
In this realm of endless flight,
Sleep's embrace feels just right.

With each breath, I touch the stars,
No more battles, no more scars.
In this journey, I am free,
In sleep's wave, I dream of me.

The Lull of Stars

As night descends, silence reigns,
The world sleeps, shedding chains.
Stars above, a quiet choir,
Singing softly, heart's desire.

In the stillness, shadows play,
Guiding dreams that drift away.
Each twinkle holds a tale,
Of whispered wishes that set sail.

Among the constellations bright,
I find comfort in the light.
A mosaic of hope and fears,
Woven softly with our tears.

The lull of stars, a sweet embrace,
Inviting calm, a sacred space.
In this night, I close my eyes,
And find myself beneath the skies.

Ethereal Slumber

In the hush of night's embrace,
Stars whisper secrets soft and low.
Wrapped in dreams, we find our place,
In shadows where the moonlight glows.

Drifting on a gentle breeze,
Lulled by nature's softest tune.
Time stands still among the trees,
As night surrenders to the moon.

Waves of calm, a tranquil stream,
Lift us high on velvet wings.
In this space, we dare to dream,
Where every heart's desire sings.

Awake, we greet the morning light,
cherishing the dreams we've spun.
Ethereal slumber fades from sight,
But in our hearts, the magic runs.

Luminescent Reflections

Amidst the shadows, light will dance,
Mirrored souls in tranquil streams.
With every glance, a fleeting chance,
To glimpse the truth behind our dreams.

Ripples form as thoughts unwind,
In pools of silver, soft and bright.
The heart's desires gently bind,
In luminescent, warm delight.

Each moment shines, a fleeting spark,
Illuminating paths we tread.
In the silence, we find the arc,
Of every word that's left unsaid.

Reflections weave a tapestry,
Of the lives we've yet to know.
In luminous grace, we'll wander free,
With wisdom gained from all we sow.

Heavenly Horizons

Beneath the sky where dreams take flight,
Horizons stretch, a canvas wide.
Golden rays of morning light,
Guide us forth, where hopes abide.

In the azure, our spirits soar,
With every step, the earth we kiss.
Embracing all we long for more,
In nature's touch, we find our bliss.

Mountains rise, their peaks adorned,
With whispers of the stars above.
Through valleys rich, and fields, we're warmed,
By the gentle hands of love.

Together, we will chase the dawn,
As day unfolds in colors rare.
In heavenly horizons drawn,
We'll paint a world beyond compare.

The Dream Weaver's Path

A tapestry of thoughts entwined,
Threads of silver, shadows cast.
In the loom of night, we find,
The dream weaver's spell is cast.

With every stitch, a tale unfolds,
Of worlds unseen and hearts afire.
In whispered winds, the story molds,
A dance of fate, a woven choir.

Wandering through the dusky fields,
Where echoes of the past will play.
The heart, a compass that reveals,
The path where dreams will light the way.

As dawn breaks forth with vibrant grace,
The threads of night will gently fray.
Yet still we tread this sacred space,
The dream weaver leads us, come what may.

Cosmic Cradle

In the dark where wonders dwell,
Stars weave tales that softly swell.
Galaxies spin in silent grace,
Cosmic whispers fill the space.

Moonlight dances on the sea,
Embracing dreams with gentle glee.
Time drifts like a feathered breeze,
Cradled in the universe's tease.

Waves of stardust touch the night,
Guiding lost souls to the light.
Each twinkle tells a story true,
In the cradle, dreams renew.

Close your eyes and feel the sway,
The cosmos hums a lullaby.
In this cradle, hearts align,
Eternity's fabric, pure divine.

The Night's Gentle Embrace

As the sun bows to the moon,
Shadows dance, a dulcet tune.
Whispers float on midnight air,
Filling hearts with gentle care.

Stars flicker, a glimmering lace,
The night wraps all in soft embrace.
Dreamers gather, spirits soar,
In the silence, we explore.

Crickets sing in rhythmic rhyme,
Painting stories through the time.
Nature sleeps, the world is still,
Wrapped in magic, hearts will fill.

Embrace the night, let go of fears,
Bathe in light, dissolve your tears.
Here in shadows, life finds grace,
In the night's gentle embrace.

Slumbering Under a Celestial Dome

Beneath the vast and starry sky,
Dreams unfurl and softly fly.
Wrapped in night's tender embrace,
Slumber dances, time and space.

The universe hums a lullaby,
Calling all the wanderers nigh.
Stars blink down, a twinkling sea,
Inviting souls to float and be.

Clouds drift by like whispers mild,
In this realm, we are all wild.
Underneath the celestial dome,
Hearts find peace, and spirits roam.

Sleep now, dear, the night is kind,
In its arms, true solace find.
For in dreams, we'll sail afar,
Together, 'neath the evening star.

Stars Softly Calling

In the velvet of the night,
Stars sing softly, pure delight.
Each glimmer holds a wish to share,
Awakening dreams, a gentle flare.

Eons pass, yet here we stand,
Together in this starlit land.
Each heartbeat hums a cosmic song,
Under the heavens, we belong.

Time elongates, moments blend,
In their glow, our worries end.
Stars softly calling, hearts will heed,
In their magic, we are freed.

Listen close, let spirits rise,
In the night, watch magic guise.
The universe, a grand ballet,
Stars softly calling, come what may.

Guiding Lights in the Twilight

Soft glimmers dance on fading days,
Whispers of stars in twilight's haze.
Paths illuminated by dreams anew,
Guiding us gently, our hearts so true.

Shadows stretch as night draws near,
Beacons of hope, casting out fear.
With every step, the world unfolds,
A tapestry woven, with stories told.

Moonlight bathes the silent trees,
Rustling leaves in the gentle breeze.
Time slows down in the evening's charm,
Embraced by night, we feel its warm.

In the stillness, we find our way,
Following lights that softly sway.
Through winding roads and quiet nights,
We journey on, guided by lights.

Cradled by the Cosmos

In the vastness where silence reigns,
Stars twinkle softly, like distant trains.
Each spark a cradle, holding dreams,
Whispers of worlds, or so it seems.

Galaxies swirl in a cosmic dance,
Every glance a chance for a glance.
Floating through the celestial sea,
Cradled by wonders, wild and free.

Nebulae bloom in colors bright,
Painting the canvas of the night.
With every heartbeat, we drift along,
Embraced by the rhythm, the universe's song.

In the darkness, we find our peace,
Cradled in dreams that never cease.
Under the vastness, we stand in awe,
A tiny heartbeat, bound by the law.

Asleep Beneath the Galaxy's Gaze

Lulled by the night, the world stands still,
As dreams gather close with a tranquil thrill.
Beneath the expanse of twinkling eyes,
We drift away, where the universe lies.

Starlit whispers cradle our minds,
In slumber's embrace, the soul unwinds.
Galaxies spin in a shimmering dance,
Guiding our thoughts in a gentle trance.

The moon looks down with a silvery smile,
Watching over us, mile by mile.
In the quiet, we breathe and sway,
Asleep beneath the night's soft play.

With every star, a wish takes flight,
Carried away in the velvet night.
Secure in dreams, we wander far,
Asleep beneath the morning star.

The Serenade of Nocturnal Blessings

Night unfolds with a gentle sigh,
Crickets play where shadows lie.
In the stillness, a song is born,
The serenade of evening's adorn.

Moonbeams drift like silver threads,
Kissing the earth where silence spreads.
Each note a promise, soft and clear,
Nocturnal blessings drawing near.

Through the dark, the soft winds hum,
Nature's choir, a soothing drum.
Whispers of magic fill the air,
In every heartbeat, a promise rare.

As night deepens with every breath,
We find solace in the dance of death.
The serenade, a lullaby sweet,
Our spirits lifted, in rhythm, we meet.

Milton Keynes UK
Ingram Content Group UK Ltd.
UKHW020734301124
451807UK00019B/780

9 789916 908150